Original title:
The Beaver's Building Blocks

Editor: Jessica Elisabeth Luik
Author: Sabrina Sarvik
ISBN HARDBACK: 978-9916-86-493-7
ISBN PAPERBACK: 978-9916-86-494-4

Wonders in Wood

In the forest deep where shadows play,
Among the trees both grand and grey,
Whispers of the wind do stray,
In ancient tongues they softly sway.

The bark with secrets etched in time,
Rings of life, a silent chime,
Oaks and pines in rows align,
In this cathedral so divine.

Leaves that dance in sunlight's glow,
A canopy where dreams bestow,
Whispers tell of tales they know,
In every gust and every flow.

Roots that delve in earth's embrace,
Holding stories of this place,
Connecting life with gentle grace,
A hidden world we seldom trace.

Birds above in chorus sing,
To the woods, a living string,
Harmonies in air they fling,
Nature's choir, eternal spring.

Forest Foundations

Beneath the shade of ancient trees,
Roots weave tales in whispering leaves,
Each bough a bridge, to sky and earth,
A testament to nature's worth.

Moss and fern in twilight's glow,
We'd find secrets far below,
Branches cradle dreams and night,
Guardians of the world's delight.

Squirrels dart and owls convene,
In a world so lush and green,
Whispers carry on the breeze,
Forest's song of timeless ease.

Craftsmen by the Creek

By the creek where currents speak,
Craftsmen hone their skill unique,
Hands that sculpt with tender might,
Wood and heart in soft twilight.

Carving dreams with each swift stroke,
Birch and oak, their tales evoke,
Water's song and chisel's sound,
Harmony in craft is found.

Creation flows like river's bend,
Nature, craftsman, each a friend,
In their hands, the forms take flight,
Through their art, the world is right.

Wood and Water Harmony

In the dance of wood and stream,
Nature weaves a living dream,
Flowing water meets stout oak,
Lush embraces in each stroke.

Ripples kiss the cedar's limbs,
Echoes of their ancient hymns,
Fish and fowl in chorus sing,
Cycles of this woodland spring.

Harmony in liquid grace,
Nature's art in every place,
Wood and water, hand in hand,
Eternal rhythm of the land.

Nature's Design Team

Nature's architects in flight,
Weave the dawn and paint the night,
Fur and feather, leaf and claw,
Each a part of forest's law.

Beavers build with tooth and wood,
In the stream where dreams once stood,
Birds nest high in crowns of green,
Crafting homes in branches keen.

From ants underfoot to bees up high,
All contribute, none deny,
Each small creature plays a part,
In the forest's boundless heart.

Nature's Carpenters

In forests deep with whispered leaves,
The beaver shapes what he believes,
With teeth like chisels, strong and true,
He crafts new paths for waters blue.

Dams arise where streams once flowed,
Nature's architect, never slowed,
By morning light and twilight's gleam,
He molds the world with gentle scheme.

Dam-Level Dedication

From dawn till dusk, their work commences,
With purpose clear, no false pretenses,
Amidst the rush of river tides,
The beavers build where secrets hide.

Wood and mud, their tools of trade,
A testament to the lives they've made,
With steadfast hearts and tireless drive,
In nature's symphony, they strive.

Masterful Timber Designs

Within the woods, a keen divide,
Where beavers ply their craft with pride,
Each branch and twig, a master's choice,
In silent work, they leave their voice.

Through seasons harsh, they hold their ground,
In snowy banks and soil unbound,
Their lodges rise with artful grace,
A testament to nature's place.

Crafted Currents

Where waters weave through vale and glen,
The beaver's touch is felt by men,
With paws and teeth, they steer the flow,
In currents shaped by hands below.

Through tranquil pools and rippling streams,
Their handiwork reflects in dreams,
In nature's heart, their legacy,
Engraved in time's vast tapestry.

Wood Whisperers of the Wild

In shadows deep where secrets lie,
The trees converse with a gentle sigh,
Their ancient stories softly told,
In whispers wild, the woods unfold.

The wind is their beloved muse,
Through leaves and branches, tales diffuse,
A symphony of rustling grace,
Embracing time, they leave no trace.

From dawn till dusk, a silent choir,
Each note a tale, each breeze a lyre,
Their wisdom flows in verdant streams,
A world alive with whispered dreams.

Sylvan Masterpieces

Upon the canvas of the Earth,
The forest breathes in silent mirth,
With every shade and hue they paint,
A masterpiece without restraint.

The palette of the morning dew,
Reflects the sunlight breaking through,
Each beam a brushstroke pure and bright,
Creating dawn from endless night.

The twilight comes with hues of gold,
Yet more spectacular art unfolds,
Beneath the moon, their craft is clear,
A gallery that knows no peer.

Building by Moonlight

When the moon takes her nightly throne,
The forest builders are unknown,
In silver beams they weave their dreams,
Constructing life by quiet streams.

Their tools are shadows, roots, and leaves,
Crafting wonders no one perceives,
Each grain of soil, each tendril green,
A testament to night unseen.

By morning light their work is shown,
To mortal eyes their toil unknown,
But in the moonlit hours, they thrive,
In moonlight's magic, they're alive.

Forest's Hydrologists

In silent groves where waters flow,
The forest's secrets gently grow,
Hydrologists of nature's art,
Their work in silence, they impart.

Stream by stream and drop by drop,
They weave their web, no halt or stop,
Through roots of oak and ferny bed,
The life-blood of the woods is spread.

From mighty rivers to mere brooks,
They carry tales in every nook,
A story told by liquid dance,
Of nature's wondrous, fluid chance.

Branch by Branch

In the hush of morning light,
Awakens the shade, gentle and bright.
Leaves whisper tales of old,
Branch by branch, their stories unfold.

From roots that delve so deep,
Silent oaths, the forest keeps.
With each dawn, a vow renewed,
In branches where life's song is brewed.

Wind's soft serenade ensues,
Caressing greens with dewy hues.
Nature's fingers trace the sky,
Branch by branch, dreams soar high.

Paws of Precision

Stealthy steps in twilight's cloak,
Under moonlight, secrets spoke.
Eyes that gleam with midnight's fire,
Paws of precision, never tire.

Graceful leaps and silent lands,
Meld with shadows, winds command.
A dance through woods with purpose clear,
Paws of precision, harbor no fear.

Mystic trails and paths unseen,
Woven threads in nature's scheme.
Every prowl a crafted art,
Paws of precision, nature's heart.

Timberland Tactician

A wise old oak stands tall,
Guardian of the forest hall.
From bark to leaf, a tale spins,
Timberland tactician begins.

Mapping paths with seasoned grace,
Through canopies, a silent chase.
Strategies in green unfurl,
Timberland tactician's world.

In echoes of the evening call,
Heed the master, heed the thrall.
Nature's chessboard, he commands,
Timberland tactician's hands.

Quaint Quarters of the Creek

In the hush where waters meet,
Ripples whisper, so discreet.
Pebbles play a gentle tune,
In quaint quarters of the creek, we swoon.

Silver minnows dart and sway,
Under sun's soft, golden ray.
Emerald banks, where secrets lie,
Quaint quarters of the creek, dreams fly.

Flowing tales in liquid sound,
Nature's peace so deeply found.
Every brook a story meek,
In quaint quarters of the creek.

Architects by the Stream

By the bubbling brook, they build their dreams,
Gentle ripples weave, whispering their schemes.
Branches bend under careful design,
A woodwork crafted, both humble and divine.

In twilight's glow, their work does stand,
Timeless creations of tiny hands.
Patterns emerge, both bold and serene,
These are the architects by the stream.

Sun and shadow play on the flowing art,
Rippling water and craft never part.
In silence they labor, nature's grand theme,
Builders of wonder, architects by the stream.

Whittled Wonders

From gnarled wood, their homes appear,
Whittled wonders, year by year.
Patient carvings on nature's canvas,
Steadfast, serene, through seasons pass.

Small hands toil, crafting with grace,
Each cut a whisper, in nature's place.
Shapes emerge from the forest old,
Stories in rings, of secrets untold.

Beneath the leaves, in shadows green,
Whittled wonders gently seen.
Silent bards of the wooded halls,
Crafting poems as the night falls.

Secret Structures of the Stream

In quiet corners, where waters meet,
Lie hidden marvels, rare and sweet.
Secret structures of the stream,
Built in silence, like a dream.

Pebbles and twigs in careful stacks,
Softly aligned along nature's tracks.
No eyes behold, yet they still stand,
Testaments crafted from gentle hands.

Mysteries flow beneath the gleam,
Forming the secret structures of the stream.
Quiet creations, unseen and serene,
Living art where none intervene.

Nature's Naval Engineers

In mossy havens, on banks they toil,
Naval engineers in native soil.
Crafting vessels of wood and twig,
Navigating rivers, lithe and sprig.

Each curve and line with purpose placed,
Echoes of nature, deftly traced.
Voyages start on life's gentle stream,
Sailing through sunlight, chasing a dream.

Structures that float and some that sink,
Born from instinct in nature's rink.
Nature's naval engineers, they steer,
Architects of water, pioneers.

Tranquil Timber Tapestry

In the heart of the verdant grove,
Whispers the oak's gentle trove,
Sunlight through a leafy sieve,
Nature's symphony, softly give.

Moss cushions the ancient roots,
Birdsong mingles, sweet pursuits,
Time moves in a slow ballet,
Here in the woods, where peace does stay.

Leaves caressing every breeze,
Branches sway with tranquil ease,
A tapestry of green so rare,
Woven with the forest air.

Flowered paths and ferny trails,
Secret spots where calm prevails,
In this haven, peace reclaim,
Nature calls us by our name.

Here, the soul finds its repair,
Wrapped in nature's tender care,
Every moment, soft, divine,
In this tranquil, timber shrine.

Echoes in the Timber

Deep within the forest's fold,
Stories ancient, yet untold,
Echoes of the time-worn bark,
Whisper softly in the dark.

Owls call out a haunting tune,
Underneath the silver moon,
Wind through trees, a murmured lull,
Timber echoes, never dull.

Footsteps soft on needles tread,
Whispers past of what was said,
Ghostly tunes by branches sung,
In the woods, where time is young.

A tale of earth, a song of sky,
Nature's lore, both low and high,
Echoes woven through the wood,
Timber's tale, misunderstood.

Mysteries of the forest deep,
Where the secrets safely sleep,
Listen close to what it shares,
Echoes in the timber cares.

Streamside Structure

By a stream's soft, gentle flow,
Life's small wonders freely grow,
Pebbles rest under the gleam,
Building dreams by nature's seam.

Ripples kiss the mossy stone,
Crafting bridges, overgrown,
Graceful arcs of woody crests,
Mother Nature's grand behests.

Roots that drink from liquid life,
Weave through rocks, avoiding strife,
Silent architects in green,
Crafting scenes serene, unseen.

Sunlight dances on the waves,
Patterns in the water, saves,
Each cascade a breath so pure,
Streamside structure's art demure.

Peace is built on flowing beams,
Brick by brick of tranquil dreams,
In this sanctuary found,
Structure in the water's sound.

Waterside Whispers

Where the waters softly drift,
Nature's whispers often sift,
Through the reeds and willow trees,
Carried by the tender breeze.

Secrets told in splashing sighs,
Echo through the dragonflies,
Rippling words from shore to shore,
Silent tales forevermore.

Shadows dance upon the lake,
Whispers speak for silence's sake,
Crickets sing their twilight hymn,
In the cool where light grows dim.

Moonbeams paint a silver hue,
Upon the waves, an argent queue,
Voices of the night arise,
Waterside with lullabies.

Listening to the midnight hush,
Where the whispered secrets rush,
In these murmured, peaceful sleeps,
Waterside a secret keeps.

Engineering Nature's Symphony

Machines in tune with whispering trees,
Blueprints drawn by nature's breeze.
Metal meets with earth's embrace,
Crafting wonders, place to place.

Rivets sing with waterfalls,
Bridges rise as morning calls.
Gears turn with a gentle hum,
Nature and tech in perfect sum.

Structures strong, both old and new,
Symphony of green and blue.
Engineers with hearts so wise,
Building dreams beneath the skies.

Nature's pulse in every part,
Blueprints born from earth's heart.
Steel and stone, and soil and sand,
Shape the world with careful hand.

Balanced scales of life and lore,
Harmony in structure's core.
From circuits fine to rivers wide,
Nature's symphony as our guide.

Riverbank Architects

By tranquil banks, where waters flow,
Architects leave footprints slow.
Designs drawn with thoughtful care,
Structures rise to meet the air.

Timber, stone, and dreams unite,
Rivers whisper through the night.
Each blueprint a poetic line,
Crafted by those who read the sign.

Flowing curves and arches tall,
Nature's blueprint guides it all.
Symbiosis of man and stream,
In every beam and every seam.

Grains of sand become our base,
Foundations set with calm and grace.
Bridges span and homes arise,
In awe beneath the open skies.

Artisans with vision keen,
Build where rivers dance and gleam.
From fertile banks, ideas spring,
Riverbank architects create and sing.

Whispers of the Dam Builder

Silent streams with whispers loud,
Dam builders work, heads unbowed.
Plans in hand with strong resolve,
Nature's force, they seek to solve.

Concrete walls and steel so strong,
Hold the river's mighty song.
Water tamed to serve our need,
Built with caution, care, and creed.

Echoes of a mountain's cry,
Resonate beneath the sky.
Builders hear, and heed the call,
Rise the structure, proud and tall.

In quiet valleys, works of art,
Dams that pulse with nature's heart.
Guardians of the flow and tide,
Balancing what's deep inside.

Builders with a vision sweet,
Harness rivers at their feet.
Whispers of the dam's refrain,
Protecting lands from storm and rain.

Creekside Carpenter's Craft

By the creek where songs are sweet,
Carpenters with rhythmic beat.
Saw and hammer, chisel too,
Crafting dreams from out the blue.

Wood and water blend as one,
Creekside beams beneath the sun.
Tambourines of nature, play,
Guiding hands at work each day.

Cottages and bridges form,
Shelter from the rain and storm.
Each fine touch a master's claim,
Creekside carpenters' acclaim.

Echoes of the forest sound,
In each plank where love is found.
Building with a heart so true,
Crafting life from nature's view.

Harmony in every grain,
Carved with care, in sun and rain.
Creekside carpenters' delight,
Crafting wonders, pure and bright.

Stream's Sculptor

In valleys deep, it carves with grace,
A steady hand in nature's race.
Through rock and soil, it winds and weaves,
A masterpiece that none believes.

With patience, time, and gentle force,
It crafts its path, its winding course.
Erosion's dance, an artful play,
Unveiling beauty day by day.

The stones it shapes, the path it clears,
The stream, a sculptor, pioneers.
Its work, though slow, forever grand,
A testament to nature's hand.

The ripples sing of art unseen,
In waters clear and forest green.
A silent artist, tireless yet,
The stream's true craft we won't forget.

Silent Symphony

The moonlight casts a silver glow,
On rippling waves that ebb and flow.
A whispering breeze through leaves does sweep,
Awaking dreams that gently creep.

The nightingale begins its song,
A tender tune both clear and long.
In shadows deep, the secrets lie,
As melodies meet sky and sigh.

Soft crickets chirp in rhythmic rhyme,
A silent symphony in time.
Each note, a thread in evening's weave,
A haunting sound, a sigh, a heave.

The stars, like notes on velvet black,
Compose a song, no soul can lack.
As night unfolds its tender strains,
A symphony in silent reigns.

Forest Architects

The beavers build with careful grace,
In twilight's soft, enchanting lace.
With bark and branch, their homes arise,
Beneath the watch of midnight skies.

Each dam they craft, a fortress strong,
A structure that will last long.
The forest hums with life and sound,
Where nature's architects are found.

The woodlands teem with subtle skill,
As creatures work with quiet will.
From burrows deep to nests on high,
Their labor framed against the sky.

In mossy glens, their plans emerge,
With streams and trees that softly surge.
These architects, both small and grand,
Shape the contours of the land.

Waterside Artists

By riverside, they paint and craft,
With flora bright and shadows daft.
Their palettes rich with every hue,
Creating scenes of verdant view.

The lilies bloom like stars in ponds,
Reflecting skies in silent bonds.
With reeds and rushes, their brush strokes fine,
They capture moments, scenes divine.

The frogs compose their evening calls,
A chorus by the water's walls.
Each note, a mark upon the dusk,
A soundscape rich, a feeling husk.

The dragonflies in shimmering flight,
Sketch arcs of day in morning light.
Waterside artists blend and meld,
A living canvas, beauty held.

Wild Engineers

With branches torn, and leaves so bright,
They build their homes, from dawn till night.
Nature's architects, in streams they thrive,
Their dams create a world alive.

In quiet woodlands, they make their mark,
With silent skills, and hearts so stark.
Diligence drives them, day by day,
Creating paths where waters sway.

Their teeth like tools, so sharp and keen,
Shaping the land, in every scene.
The world transforms by their great might,
Crafting beauty with pure delight.

In every corner, their tales are spun,
Against the backdrop of setting sun.
Unseen, yet felt, in each terrain,
Echoes of their work remain.

These creatures small, with purpose grand,
Mold the rivers, shape the land.
In harmony they live and grow,
Ingenious in the ebb and flow.

Streamside Silhouettes

Beside the stream, in evening's glow,
Silhouettes in twilight show.
Graceful forms, in shadows cast,
Moments fleeting, never last.

Willows whisper, water's hum,
A symphony where night's begun.
Shapes of night, in moonlit schemes,
Silent guardians of our dreams.

Ripples dance on silvered skin,
Where night and nature blend within.
Each silhouette, a story told,
Of hidden life, both young and old.

Crickets sing and owls take flight,
In this mystic, tranquil night.
Streamside shades, with secrets deep,
Promises they vow to keep.

In these darkened, peaceful sights,
Find the magic in the nights.
Ephemeral, yet so serene,
In this wondrous, quiet scene.

Pioneer of the Pond

In silent pools where lilies lay,
The pioneer of ponds holds sway.
Amid the reeds, where waters gleam,
He builds his world, an endless dream.

From muddy depths with patient care,
Constructs his home, beyond compare.
A fortress made of twigs and earth,
A marvel of creative birth.

His ripples spread through waters clear,
A symphony for all who hear.
He shapes his realm with steady hand,
A ruler of this tranquil land.

Dawn to dusk, persistent strife,
He carves his niche, he molds his life.
Unyielding spirit, pure resolve,
Around his will, the waters revolve.

In solitude, his legacy,
A testament for all to see.
To nature's call, he does respond,
The tireless pioneer of the pond.

Wooded Wonders

In forest depths where shadows play,
Woodland wonders lead the way.
Creatures whisper tales untold,
Of ancient lore and hearts of bold.

Beneath the canopy so green,
Life unfolds in hidden scene.
Trees stand tall, with whispers heard,
Nature's voice in every word.

The dappled light on fern and moss,
Mirrors dance the paths they cross.
In each corner, life's embrace,
Holds the forest's secret grace.

Foxes dart and deer do tread,
Through the paths where leaves are spread.
Silent footsteps, gentle glides,
In the woods where peace resides.

Woodland wonders, pure and bright,
Craft a world in nature's light.
In their midst, we find our place,
Within the wild, a soft embrace.

Tales of Timber and Water

Upon the stream where branches dip,
With wooden tales so fine,
Nature's hand in timber's script,
Weaves stories line by line.

The whispers of the rustling leaves,
Dance gently with the breeze,
In shadows where the river weaves,
Through ancient forest trees.

Here where time feels slow and kind,
And waters hum a song,
In harmony, trees and rivers bind,
Tales where they belong.

Each ripple tells a storied past,
With timber old and wise,
A legacy that long will last,
Beneath the open skies.

So listen close to water's sound,
To timbers that stand tall,
In every drop and every pound,
A tale told by them all.

Natures Marvelous Constructor

The beaver with its clever mind,
Constructs with steady flair,
A fortress where its kind will find,
A refuge free of care.

With teeth that carve through bark and wood,
It builds a sturdy dam,
Engineering what it could,
From nature's open hand.

No blueprint needed for its art,
Instincts guide its way,
A marvel of each forest part,
In night as well as day.

Waters flow hold secrets kept,
By beaver's careful craft,
Creating homes where life is swept,
Along a gentle draft.

In awe we watch the builder's grace,
As nature's plans unfold,
A masterpiece in every place,
The beaver's tales are told.

Waterside Woodwork

By river's edge where tall trees stand,
An artisan at work,
With nimble paws and crafted hand,
No tasks does it shirk.

It fells the mighty timber down,
To build its cozy home,
In waters deep it will not drown,
But gently through them roam.

Crafting lodges warm and tight,
With sticks and mud and leaves,
It works both day and night,
In structures it believes.

Each log set with a purpose strong,
To guard against the tide,
Ensuring it won't go wrong,
In life by waterside.

So marvel at this woodwork true,
By nature's own design,
Where water's edge meets timber's hue,
In perfect, grand align.

Mysteries Under the Dam

Below the dam where shadows play,
Secrets hide in deep,
In water's murky, quiet sway,
Where creatures softly creep.

A labyrinth of chambers dark,
Lit by filtered light,
Where mysteries leave a subtle mark,
In whispers of the night.

The current tells a quiet tale,
Of life's enduring spark,
In silences, no voice to pale,
Beneath the beaver's mark.

A world in dusk and twilight hue,
Of wonders and of awe,
Beneath the water's gentle blue,
Nature's timeless law.

In hidden spots where few have seen,
Life plays its secret game,
Where water's magic, clear and keen,
Speaks whispers in a name.

Lodge of Silent Architects

In shadows where the river winds,
The beavers shape and dream,
With careful tooth and quiet mind,
They craft their hidden theme.

Their lodges rise in twilight dim,
Where moonlight gently plays,
An ode to nature's whispered hymn,
In tranquil, silvered rays.

Each branch they place with silent skill,
A testament of lore,
In harmony with stream and hill,
Their artistry does soar.

Through seasons' ebb and flow they thrive,
In secret wood-built spires,
Their legacy, both fierce and live,
Ignites our still desires.

To marvel at their deft design,
Is to see a world renewed,
By the Lodge of Silent Architects,
In nature's quietude.

Beneath the Wooden Towers

Beneath the wooden towers tall,
Where rivers gently bend,
There flows a life both quaint and small,
Yet to the world, a friend.

Among the roots and woven beams,
A haven comes alive,
The murmurs of their thoughtful schemes,
With purpose they contrive.

The current hums a gentle tune,
As creatures move with care,
In shadows soft beneath the moon,
Their stories dance in air.

In tunnels deep and pathways grand,
Their homes are wreathed in leaves,
A testament to nature's hand,
And all that it achieves.

Beneath the wooden towers' shade,
An ecosystem blooms,
In quiet, tender plans they've made,
Life's symphony resumes.

Riparian Blueprint

Upon the river's gentle clasp,
A world begins to mold,
With tiny paws and tender grasp,
A blueprint to behold.

The water sings its endless song,
As busy hands lay claim,
To build, to shape, to right the wrong,
And bring forth nature's fame.

In patterns rich with ancient lore,
They plant each wooden beam,
A testament to craft and more,
In every flowing stream.

Through sunlit days and starry nights,
Their vision comes to life,
In hidden depths and layered heights,
A haven free from strife.

The riparian dream takes flight,
In webs of branch and vine,
A blueprint of harmonious might,
In water's grand design.

Ecosystem Engineers

With gentle strokes and whispered care,
The beavers carve their place,
In waters calm or rivers where,
Their works of art they trace.

Solid architects of pond and stream,
With patience they create,
An ecosystem's silent dream,
In which lives animate.

Their dams a balance do maintain,
Of water's ebb and flow,
Gifting life where droughts may reign,
And verdant landscapes grow.

Each gnaw and notch a testament,
To nature's grand design,
A synergy so eloquent,
Where earth and water bind.

O engineers with humble hand,
Your legacy endures,
In every thriving, rippled land,
Your spirit still assures.

Eden's Engineers

In twilight's gentle, hushed retreat,
Where rivers whisper, shadows meet,
Craftsmen of dusk in quiet bays,
Sing softly of their woodland ways.

Inwoven dreams of twig and earth,
A symphony of dam's rebirth,
Nature's architects, silent shapers,
Artistry in night's vapor papers.

Echoing their ancient creed,
With every branch and bough decreed,
Builders of this sacred glen,
Guardians of the beaver's den.

Moonlight glints on rippled streams,
Cradles visions, wildest dreams,
Masoned realms where life begins,
Cyphers of old forest hymns.

Beneath the starlit canopy,
Eden's engineers roam free,
Weaving life through waters pure,
Elder tales they do ensure.

Craftsmen of the Creek

On creek's soft edge, where silence sings,
Master architects spin their rings,
In ripples' mirror, visions clear,
Etched in twilight, closely near.

Whispers of water, dusk unfolds,
Enchanting tales, time gently holds,
Craftsmen weave with deft intent,
Ancient secrets softly sent.

Builders of tales in thread and stone,
Echoing in a silent tone,
Their homes are drawn in nature's hand,
Ever shaping, 'cross the land.

Twigs and leaves in fingers deft,
Fortresses and castles left,
Beside the creek, in dusky shade,
A world entwined by craft and trade.

Mystic places sewn by night,
Beneath the moon's celestial light,
Craftsmen of the creek arise,
Art in essence, nature's guise.

Crafting Nature's Barricades

By flowing banks, a dance ensues,
Nature's builders with their cues,
Crafting softly, shades of night,
In whispers of the soft moonlight.

With branches, twigs, and patient hands,
They carve their dreams in silent lands,
Barrier 'gainst the wildest tide,
In harmony with stars as guide.

Through thickets dense, their tales they weave,
In faith, their strength they do believe,
Nature's fort in tranquil scribe,
Woven deep in stream's own vibe.

In water's lull, their purpose found,
In rhythms of the earthen ground,
Guardians of the flow, they stand,
Ever still on nature's grand.

At twilight's touch, they shape anew,
With every breath, the water's view,
Crafting nature's barricades,
In hushed forest, light that fades.

Shapers of the Streamside

Beneath the canopy so green,
Work shapers in a world serene,
Their hands move deftly, carved in bark,
Stories held in waters dark.

Through twilight hours, unseen craft,
In every branch and every raft,
Silent artists, soft twilight's hue,
Shaping dreams, the dawn anew.

Nature's sculptors, firm yet kind,
Building worlds with ease of mind,
Streamside whispers in the night,
Guiding hands with nature's light.

Waters flow in tender dance,
With each ripple, life's romance,
Shapers mold, and thus they stay,
In realms where wild spirits play.

Silent shadows, streamside's song,
Echoes of their work prolong,
Makers of the twilight's glide,
Guardians by the riverside.

Mastery of the Maple

In autumn's golden embrace,
Leaves flutter in the breeze,
Maple's majesty in place,
Nature's calm, eternal ease.

Roots grip the ancient earth,
Bark whispers tales untold,
Seasons cycle, rebirth,
Through the ages proud and bold.

Sap flows like liquid gold,
A sweet life's hidden muse,
Branches in patterns unfold,
A tapestry of hues.

Sunlight dances on leaves,
Casting shadows below,
In its splendor, one believes,
In the world's gentle flow.

Each seed a silent story,
Of life, love, and the sky,
In the maple's timeless glory,
Nature's secrets lie.

Crafters of the Creek

Water whispers to the stones,
Secrets from upstream,
In each ripple, life is shown,
In every sunlit gleam.

Hands of nature, ever true,
Shaping sand and clay,
Crafters old, but always new,
Singing night and day.

Fish dart in the crystal flow,
Where shadows dance and play,
The creek where all life does grow,
In its own subtle way.

Willows kiss the water's edge,
Their leaves in whispers speak,
Nature crafts a living pledge,
Down the timeless creek.

Each bend a newfound story,
Each turn a whispered rhyme,
In the creek, life finds glory,
Crafting art through time.

Marshalling the Marshlands

Where reeds and lilies stand tall,
Marshlands stretch out wide,
Herons echo nature's call,
On the rippling tide.

Water laps at silent shores,
Vast fields of verdant green,
Life in hidden corridors,
In the twilight serene.

Frogs croak in the dusky light,
Crickets sing the night's hymn,
Marshlands marshalling the night,
In shadows deep and slim.

Morning mist upon the rise,
Veils of silver and gold,
Nature's canvas in disguise,
Stories of life retold.

Marshalling the marshland's grace,
Every dawn a rebirth,
Nature's quiet, gentle pace,
A testament to earth.

Sylvan Sculptors

In the heart of ancient woods,
Sylvan sculptors dwell,
Crafting dreams of leafy hoods,
In their quiet shell.

Roots entwine in hidden art,
Branches reach the sky,
Every tree, a work of heart,
In nature's gentle sigh.

Oak and birch, a silent blend,
Sculpting shadows, light,
Nature's artists without end,
Crafting day and night.

Sunlight pierces through the leaves,
Patterns on the ground,
Woods where every spirit weaves,
A magic so profound.

Sylvan sculptors of the earth,
In the forest deep,
Carving beauty, life, and mirth,
In a timeless sweep.

Riparian Residences

By the rushing river's edge,
Where reeds and willows sigh,
Creatures build their hidden homes,
Beneath the open sky.

The water sings its endless song,
A lullaby so sweet,
As fish and frogs find refuge there,
In cool and quiet retreat.

Dragonflies dance on the breeze,
Their wings a blur of light,
Among the rippling, silver waves,
That shimmer in the night.

In the shelter of the rocks,
Crabs scuttle to and fro,
Each nook and cranny filled with life,
In nature's ebb and flow.

Riparian homes, a world complete,
Where harmony abounds,
A sanctuary for all to share,
Within its gentle bounds.

Forest Engineers

Among the towering, ancient pines,
The beavers work with glee,
Crafting dams of sticks and stones,
To tame the wild spree.

Their teeth so sharp, their focus keen,
They sculpt the flowing streams,
Creating ponds and wetlands deep,
For nature's vibrant dreams.

With every twig and every branch,
They weave a sturdy frame,
Transforming landscapes with their skill,
In a masterful acclaim.

The forest hums with songs of life,
In waters calm and clear,
Thanks to the engineers of wood,
Who hold the wild dear.

Beavers build with patient hands,
A realm both safe and free,
In the heart of woodland depths,
A testament to liberty.

Whittling Wonders

Underneath the canopy green,
The squirrels whittle with delight,
Carving through the nuts and seeds,
Hidden from the light.

Their tiny paws like sculptor's tools,
Shape each precious prize,
In the whispering woodland glades,
Beneath the endless skies.

Woodpeckers join the rhythmic dance,
Their beaks a chisel fine,
Carving out the insect trails,
Along the bark's rough line.

Nature's artists, deft and true,
Creatures great and small,
Whittling wonders day by day,
In the forest hall.

Each tap and scrape, a melody,
Within the green embrace,
Creating intricate designs,
In nature's timeless grace.

Nature's Blueprints

Within the earthly blueprint grand,
Lies a secret, wise and old,
Patterns etched by time and tide,
In stories yet untold.

From spirals in a nautilus shell,
To leaves in perfect rows,
Nature drafts her master plots,
In every petal that grows.

Fractals in the mountain's edge,
Ripples on the shore,
Signs of nature's careful hand,
Crafting ever more.

The spider spins a silken web,
Geometric and taut,
A testament to nature's art,
In every single knot.

Nature's blueprints guide us all,
In harmony's great quest,
From microcosm to the vast,
Her plans are manifest.

Tales from the Timberline

Whispers weave through the pines,
Telling tales of ancient times,
Of creatures that carved the night,
And dreams that took to flight.

Shadows dance on the forest floor,
Echoes of legends, evermore,
In the timberline, where stories grow,
Secrets only the trees will know.

The moonlight casts a silver thread,
Binding tales that time once shed,
Nature's lore in branches' croon,
Underneath a watchful moon.

Fables flow like rivers' bends,
In the forest where the ancient mends,
Each leaf a parchment, filled with lore,
Awaiting those who seek and explore.

In the heart of the timberline,
Where past and present intertwine,
Eldritch whispers softly guide,
Through the woods, with tales to bide.

Guardians of the Ripples

In the stillness of the lake,
Where moonlight casts a gentle wake,
Guardians rise from waters deep,
Oaths of silence they shall keep.

Ripples dance in twilight's grasp,
Echoes of a timeless task,
Silent watchers in the night,
Guiding journeys by the light.

Waves of wisdom lap the shore,
Tales of ages' ancient lore,
Protectors of the tranquil deep,
Where the shadows softly sleep.

Mystery shrouds their quiet gaze,
In the ripples, moonbeam plays,
From depths unseen, they softly rise,
Guardians of the nighttime skies.

In watery realms of moonlight's gleam,
They guard the secrets of the stream,
Bound by ripples they remain,
Eternal watchers of the plane.

Crafting Canals and Lodges

With paws that sculpt the water's edge,
They build a world of branch and sedge,
Crafting canals to shape their land,
Silent builders, hand in hand.

In lodges warm, they weave their dreams,
Harnessing the forest streams,
Masters of the flowing art,
Nature's architects, set apart.

Through twilight hours, they engineer,
Paths that keep their homes secure,
In the quiet, their work abides,
A testament to nature's guides.

Canals that wind through the trees,
Homes that sway in the gentle breeze,
Every twig and every bough,
Speaks of skill and silent vow.

In forests deep, their tales are told,
Of lodgers brave and builders bold,
Crafting life from stream and wood,
In harmony with the land they've stood.

Dwellers of the Dammed Delight

In the hush of twilight's gleam,
Where the rivers weave their dream,
Dwellers form with steadfast might,
An edifice of dammed delight.

Branches bend to their command,
Waters flow at their demand,
In the twilight, shadows flit,
Where the peaceful waters sit.

Dens and lodges rise anew,
Crafted by the skillful few,
Masters of the damming art,
Building worlds set apart.

Underneath the starlit sky,
In the wilderness, they lie,
Silent keepers of the night,
Guardians of their dammed delight.

In the heart of nature's song,
Where the river's tales belong,
Dwellers of the dammed domain,
Leave their mark upon the plain.

Streamside Storytellers

Upon the banks, the waters dance,
In moonlit hues, they find their trance,
With whispered tales, they weave their song,
Of lovers lost, and dreams prolonged.

The willow leans, a mentor's grace,
To travelers with a weary face,
Its branches tell of ages past,
Where truths are held, and shadows cast.

In evening's glow, the crickets play,
Their melodies to end the day,
As fireflies script the twilight's prose,
A streamside verse that ebbs and flows.

The stones beneath, in silence wait,
To feel the stories they create,
For every ripple, every wave,
Holds voices of the brave and saved.

So gather close, by waters clear,
These ancient tales, we hold them dear,
For by the stream, where dreams are spun,
The storytellers' work is never done.

Architects of the Wild

In forests deep, where shadows play,
The architects of wild survey,
With paw and claw, they shape the land,
A symphony, at their command.

The beaver builds with tireless might,
A fortress strong by moon's pale light,
While birds weave nests in lofty trees,
Their mastery swayed by the breeze.

The wolves patrol their hidden trails,
With silent steps and murmured tales,
Their eyes reflect the ancient lore,
Of territories to explore.

The ants below, in endless file,
Construct their homes in patient style,
Each grain of earth, a task complete,
A testament to their conceit.

Nature's architects, in roles so vast,
Their legacies through eons cast,
In every nook, and branch, and leaf,
Their art brings solace and belief.

Timber Whispers

Among the pines, a secret breath,
The timber whispers, still as death,
In groves where ancient roots run deep,
The forest's silent vigils keep.

Each birch and oak, with weathered scars,
Holds memories of distant stars,
Their bark recounts the passage fair,
Of seasons' dance and nature's care.

In twilight's hush, the breezes sing,
A chorus of the forest king,
Their rustling leaves, a soft refrain,
Of whispered joy and timeless pain.

The trunks conversing, low and slow,
Of tales the woodland creatures know,
Their murmurs blend, a grand design,
In timbered halls so old, divine.

So wander where the shadows fall,
And listen to their whispered call,
For in the heart of timbered realms,
The whispers guide, and overwhelm.

Pondside Professionals

Beside the pond, in tranquil scene,
Professionals in silence glean,
The heron stands with practiced grace,
In patient watch, a poised embrace.

The frog, with knowing eyes so wide,
In lily's shade, does deftly hide,
A leap away from dragonfly,
Their worlds aligned beneath the sky.

The turtles bask on sunlit logs,
In calm rapport with whims of frogs,
Their wisdom, etched in shells of time,
Speaks softly of the pond's old rhyme.

The ripples spread with gentle nudge,
Each movement made without a grudge,
For here, professionals align,
In harmony, their fates entwine.

Beside the pond, where peace resides,
Their work unfolds with nature's tides,
A testament to lives well spun,
By pondside pros beneath the sun.

Whispers of the Dam

Below the moon's faint, silvery gleam,
Whispers rise like vapor's dream.
Ancient stones and flowing streams,
Hold the secrets, hidden schemes.

Echoes drift in midnight's veil,
Tell the tales beyond the pale.
Silent guardians, never frail,
Their murmurs in the night prevail.

Mystic shadows dance and play,
On water's edge where spirits sway.
Guarding realms till break of day,
In whispers, prayers softly lay.

Time's old secrets, ages fold,
Stories lost, and legends told.
In the dam's embrace, controlled,
Whispers weave, a silent gold.

Reverence in each ripple found,
Nature's pulse, a ghostly sound.
Whispers of the dam resound,
In the heart, forever bound.

Woodland Engineers

Crafted by claw and wooden mind,
Architects in nature find.
Bridges, tunnels, paths aligned,
By beaver teeth, the streams refined.

In twilight's hush, their work proceeds,
Silent plans where water leads.
Each twig a dream, each branch succeeds,
In shaping lands with mindful deeds.

Cedar, birch, and alder bend,
To secrets that these builders send.
Whispering woods where dreams extend,
And forest life will not contend.

A symphony of gnaw and night,
With moonlit pools, reflections bright.
These engineers craft pure delight,
Their legacy, a beaver's rite.

In amber glow of setting sun,
Work of paws is never done.
Through every stream their talent spun,
Nature's architects, second to none.

Timber Dreams

In slumber lands, where trees converse,
Timber dreams in silent verse.
Whispers of the forest nurse,
Life to aspirations terse.

Each autumn leaf a memory,
Of summers past and winters spree.
In timber dreams, the soul is free,
To wander wild, eternally.

Roots entwine in story's thread,
While treetops hum above a bed.
Of emerald canopies widespread,
Where dreams of timber softly spread.

Moonlight sifts through hazy limbs,
Dancing with the forest hymns.
Timber dreams in twilight swims,
In echoes of the night's soft trims.

Awake to whispers of the day,
Where timber dreams shall softly lay.
Guiding hearts along love's way,
In nature's arms we gently sway.

Ripple's Edge

By river's edge where echoes stir,
Whispers dance and dreams confer.
Ripples speak without demur,
In liquid tales that won't deter.

Each wave a journey, old and new,
A story in the water's blue.
By ripple's edge, the secrets grew,
Silent depths of what is true.

Reflections play on mirror's face,
Ephemeral in time and space.
Each ripple's life a fleeting trace,
Of ancient whispers' soft embrace.

In gentle hush of morning's breath,
Ripples chart the endless breadth.
Of mysteries bound in water's cleft,
Where life and dream are deftly left.

Eternal dance of wave and shore,
In ripple's edge we find much more.
A symphony of water's lore,
Forever whispered, evermore.

Forest Frameworks

In shadows green, the trunks arise,
A canopy against the skies,
Where whispers trace the ancient wood,
And roots are anchored, understood.

Leaves murmur tales of time gone by,
While branches craft their lullaby,
In silent strength, the forest stands,
Its wisdom held within its hands.

Through dappled light the pathways weave,
Where spirits walk and dreams believe,
As sunlight plays its fleeting game,
On mossy floors without a name.

Each tree a part of grand design,
Their lives entwine, their fates align,
A symphony of earth and air,
Creating structures free of care.

Together bound in nature's frame,
They hold the secrets without claim,
Forest frameworks, strong and pure,
A testament that will endure.

Rippling Residences

Across the ripples, homes are born,
From dawn's first light to misty morn,
Where echoes of the water's hymn,
Craft residences soft and trim.

The mirrored sky, a fleeting guest,
With tranquil waves, the pond is blessed,
Reflections dance with gentle grace,
In this aquatic dwelling place.

Amid the reeds where silver gleams,
Nature paints its living dreams,
An artistry in liquid form,
Where life's embrace is safe and warm.

Each ripple tells a silent tale,
Of timeless journeys, winds that sail,
Among the currents, life prevails,
In detailed homes, as spring unveils.

These residences fluid, free,
A testament to what shall be,
In ripples, dwellings intertwine,
A liquid life, pure and divine.

Shaping the Stream

The stream carves paths through ancient stone,
A melody in undertone,
With every twist, its waters write,
A chronicle of day and night.

The pebbles dance beneath its flow,
Each one a part of tales that grow,
And as the years the stream must wend,
Its shaping hand will never end.

Through valleys deep and forests bright,
The stream reflects the mountain's might,
In gentle curves or torrents strong,
It sings the earth a timeless song.

With every bend, a story told,
Of life's embrace both young and old,
Where nature's touch on waters sleek,
Creates a language pure and meek.

Shaping life by constant dream,
The steady path, a guiding beam,
In waters clear or shadows gleam,
We find the truth within the stream.

Woodland Wonders

In glades where sunlight filters down,
Nature weaves its verdant gown,
Where ferns unfurl and flowers bloom,
An endless cycle, life's perfume.

The woodland whispers ancient lore,
Of creatures past and sights galore,
Each rustling leaf, a tale to tell,
In this green sanctuary's spell.

Beneath the boughs, the secrets hide,
Where subtle streams in shadows bide,
The pulse of life in every blade,
A wondrous, ever-blooming glade.

The forest floor, a canvas wide,
With mushrooms, moss, paths side by side,
In every scent, a memory,
Of timeless growth, of boundless glee.

Through woodland wonders, we may find,
A part of nature intertwined,
In awe, we breathe and deeply know,
The magic that these woods bestow.

Canopy Craftsmen

High above in leafy spires,
Squirrels leap through breezy airs,
Weaving nests with nimble wires,
Crafted with a tender care.

Amidst the birch and oaken might,
Where sun and shadows intertwine,
Craftsmen in their daily plight,
Chisel twigs and barbs so fine.

From morning mist to twilight's call,
Their artistry is nature's song,
Echoes through each tree and hall,
In this realm where they belong.

With tails as brushes, paws as tools,
Each branch adorned with vibrant flair,
By rules of ancient woodland schools,
Their legacy hangs in the air.

Upon high breezes, watch them glide,
Masters of the canopy,
Beneath the vast and azure sky,
In a dance so wild and free.

Tranquil Timber Craft

Silent whispers, forest deep,
Wooden beams in shadows sleep,
Hand of time and nature too,
Sculpting forms within the yew.

Carvers of the very soul,
Craft their visions, make them whole,
Timber speaks in rings of age,
History upon this stage.

Calm the workshops of the woods,
Where each peg and joint is good,
Masters of the soft and hard,
Building dreams in green facades.

Tranquil moments in the pines,
Where the heart of wood entwines,
With the spirit of the land,
Shaped and touched by steady hand.

Echoed through the glade so still,
Is the love and timeless skill,
Of those who with patience grand,
Craft their art from earth and sand.

Builders of the Wild

In the heart of forest green,
By streams and fields unseen,
Wildlife architects arise,
Molding homes beneath the skies.

Beavers sculpt their water halls,
With dams and lodges, timber walls,
Otters form their river gates,
Nature's seamless architects.

High on cliffs, the eagles soar,
Nesting realms on craggy moors,
Clever foxes, burrow deep,
In earth's embrace, they safely sleep.

Each creature weaves a tapestry,
In living wild, so wild and free,
Designs perfected, nature's pride,
Builders on the great divide.

From dens in roots, to aeries high,
They craft and build beneath the sky,
Symbiosis, life's grand dream,
In the wild, a seamless scheme.

Streamside Symphony

By the babbling brook's embrace,
Water weaves a peaceful lace,
Frogs and fish in liquid dance,
Nature's flow, an endless trance.

Willows weep with gentle grace,
Casting shadows, cool the space,
Dragonflies in shimmering flight,
Day to dawn and then to night.

Birds that sing the sweetest tune,
Echo deep in afternoon,
Harmony of flowing sound,
Life's symphony all around.

In this place where waters kiss,
Sunlight sparks, a fleeting bliss,
Moments drift like fallen leaves,
In a peace no heart deceives.

Tune of life, so pure, so free,
Symphony by stream and tree,
Nature's score, both bold and grand,
In a timeless, tranquil land.

Tranquil Builders

In dawn's first light and dusk's warm fade,
With silent steps in forest glade,
Builders' hands of time employ,
To craft the world with artful joy.

Their touch as soft as morning mist,
Each creation, nature-kissed,
Yet firm as mountain's silent might,
Tranquil builders shape the night.

Oceans whisper to the shore,
Secrets whispered, evermore,
By streams and fields, by ancient trees,
Their work unravels mysteries.

They labor by the moon's soft glow,
In shadows only few will know,
Their quiet art begets the dawn,
And echoes long after they're gone.

What grows from tranquil builders' hands,
Will echo through the timeless lands,
For peace and calm, their every ply,
Builds a world that will not die.

Engineering in the Wild

In forests vast and deserts wide,
Where fierce and gentle worlds collide,
Wild engineers construct with grace,
A living, breathing interface.

Spider webs and beaver dams,
Nests that cradle, dens that host,
Each crafted by a master hand,
In nature's architectural boast.

Branch and bough, in pattern true,
They build a world anew,
Honeycombs and avian homes,
Silent hymns of nature's loams.

Beneath the stars, their plans unfold,
Reflections of innovations bold,
Silent architects of the wild,
Blueprints formed by earth's own child.

Nature's code in fibers spun,
Each work beneath the golden sun,
By creatures small and great alike,
Drawing life from nature's pike.

Symbiotic Structures

In layers fine, the lichen grows,
Across the bark, in hidden rows,
A partnership, in every cell,
A mutual tale, the trees do tell.

Fungi beneath, in soil deep,
Threads their secrets, roots they keep,
Exchange of life, a silent trade,
A complex network, nature made.

Leaves filter light, through canopy dense,
A dance of shadows, green and immense,
In sun and shade, they find their way,
Building a world, in night and day.

The wind whispers, in rustling leaves,
Secrets the forest, quietly weaves,
Symbiosis, in every breath,
Life's grand design, defying death.

If we listen, we'll hear the song,
Of symbiotic, nature strong,
A lesson taught, in structures small,
Where every life, finds room to sprawl.

Furry Foreman's Folly

In fields of green, with whiskers bright,
The foreman toils, from day to night,
With tiny paws, and keen intent,
A busy life, in effort spent.

Through tunnels deep, and meadows wide,
He digs and builds, with endless pride,
Each burrow made, each blade of grass,
A testament, to work en masse.

Yet folly lies, in over-zeal,
A price to pay, for fervent feel,
For sometimes haste, can lead astray,
A hurried heart, will find delay.

But in his eyes, a flame persists,
A spark of will, that can't desist,
To learn from fault, and rise again,
The tale of effort, thus ordained.

So furry friends, both near and far,
Take heed of lessons, from his jar,
For every dig, and every goal,
Teaches the heart, and strengthens the soul.

Woodsy Water Walls

Amidst the forest, streams do flow,
In quiet ripples, soft and slow,
Where water carves, through root and stone,
A liquid path, that's all its own.

The walls of wood, on either side,
Stand tall and dark, a nature's pride,
They hum a tune, in whispers sweet,
An ancient song, in rhythms neat.

Fish dart and weave, in currents mild,
Their silver scales, both tame and wild,
In this embrace, of wood and wave,
A sanctuary, the waters gave.

The sun breaks through, in beams of gold,
Caressing leaves, in stories told,
In every drop, a life does gleam,
A dance of light, a forest dream.

By water walls, the whispers grow,
Of time and life, in ebb and flow,
A harmony, of earth and stream,
A wooden world, in nature's scheme.

Ripples Among Timber

In shaded groves, where silence dwells,
The timbers stand, as nature tells,
Of ripples cast, in pools of light,
A gentle grace, in day and night.

Above the ground, where roots entwine,
There's life unseen, in paths divine,
Beneath the bark, stories unfold,
Of seasons new, and ages old.

Each woodland step, each quiet tread,
Stirs echoes soft, from pasts unsaid,
The forest breathes, in calm refrain,
In every leaf, a soft sustain.

The ripples spread, from branch to root,
A symphony, both deep and mute,
Where rustling leaves, like whispers fall,
A silent dance, by nature's call.

Among the trees, in tranquil air,
We find the peace, from life's despair,
For in the woods, there lies a song,
Of endless time, enduring strong.

Flowing Tapestry

Threads of memory weave gentle light,
In the loom of dawn, colors take flight,
Time's whispers stitch moments so bright,
A flowing tapestry through day and night.

Silent echoes in the brocade lay,
Glimmers of gold in twilight's sway,
Mysteries in each intricate array,
Bound by threads of life and play.

From tangled dreams a pattern spun,
Woven stories beneath the sun,
In this fabric, all hearts are one,
Infinite strands never to be undone.

Softest touch and vibrant hue,
Fingers dance in creative dew,
In every thread, a tale anew,
A flowing tapestry of me and you.

In starlit gleam and shadowed seam,
Paths converge as light does beam,
Holding close each precious dream,
In this flowing tapestry, our soul's stream.

Woodland Creations

Under branches, a realm unfolds,
In tender shade, stories are told,
Mossy carpet, emerald holds,
Life breathes gentle in hues of gold.

Creepers climb with silent grace,
Around the trunks, in warm embrace,
Ferns unfurl in secret place,
In woodland's heart, we find our space.

Whispers in the leaves above,
Echo songs of endless love,
Nature's canvas, hand in glove,
Home to feather, beast, and dove.

Creations born of root and sky,
In intricate patterns twine and tie,
Beneath the watch where tall oaks vie,
Woodland's wonders never die.

Winds weave through this sacred hall,
Answering spring's awakening call,
In woodland paths, where spirits fall,
Nature's canvas binds us all.

Streamside Structure

Bubbles dance in playful glide,
Over pebbles, currents bide,
Streamside secrets in waters wide,
Nature's architecture side by side.

Ripples sketch on liquid plane,
Etching lines in sweet refrain,
With every twist, the nymphs retain,
Streamside magic, pure and sane.

Roots dip down from canopy high,
Sipping life as years pass by,
Their woven arches touch the sky,
Embraced by streams that never lie.

Reflections hold the skies within,
Mirror worlds where dreams begin,
Streamside murmurs, nature's twin,
Flowing freely from heart to skin.

Sunbeams dance on sparkling bows,
Caressing banks where softness grows,
In streamside structure, beauty shows,
Endless rhythm that gently flows.

Calm Constructions

Built in whispers, strong yet light,
Foundations laid in silent night,
Calm constructions take their flight,
Balance found in pure delight.

Bricks of dream and beams of thought,
Pieced together where peace is sought,
Every line intricately wrought,
In calm constructions, battles fought.

Windows open to skies serene,
Doors unlock where souls convene,
Each room veiled in tranquil sheen,
Calm constructions, life between.

Pillars new as moments sway,
Holding hopes and fears at bay,
In this structure, soft pillows lay,
Guiding hearts where they may stray.

In stillness rise, these walls of grace,
Calm constructions find their space,
A refuge from the world's fast pace,
Built in peace, our safe embrace.

Mystic Dam Builders

By twilight's glow on quiet streams,
Beavers craft their timbered dreams.
With gnaw and notch, their homes arise,
In water's hush 'neath twilight skies.

Nature's engineers, so grand and small,
Their homes stand strong through winter's call.
With tales of ancient forests old,
They build in silence, brave and bold.

A gentle splash, a ripple's play,
Marks where the dam builders stay.
Guardians of the woodland's heart,
In waters safe, they each play a part.

Under crescent moon's embrace,
Dams fortify their forest's place.
Through storms and drought, they persevere,
Silent whispers echo near.

In realms where wild rivers gleam,
Beavers craft their ageless dream.
Nature's tale, in wood and stream,
A mystic dance, forever seen.

Pioneer Carpenters

In forest deep, where echoes sleep,
Pioneers their vigil keep.
With axe and saw, through ancient wood,
They fashion life where none once stood.

The sun of dawn, with golden hue,
Guides their hands in rugged view.
Cabins rise 'neath towering trees,
Sheltered safe from winter's freeze.

Cedar scents and pine wood's grain,
Frame a tale of hope and gain.
Timbered walls and sturdy beams,
Cloak their dreams in morning gleams.

Through frost and thaw, in strife and peace,
Their work commands the wild's release.
In rustic homes of skill and care,
Their legacy breathes mountain air.

By firelight's dance, their stories told,
Of days of yore and builders bold.
Pioneer hearts, both strong and grand,
Carpenters of this wondrous land.

Tales of Timbered Havens

Between the pines, where shadows play,
Rise timbered havens day by day.
Crafted with hands both skilled and sure,
Homes that stand, time's test endure.

Stories whispered in the bark,
Of settlers' hope, their spirit's spark.
Each beam and post a living tale,
Of dreams that weathered every gale.

Eaves that shelter, hearths that warm,
Timber speaks through every storm.
Guarding secrets, shadows blend,
In havens where the wilds mend.

Birdsong greets each newborn dawn,
In these homes where hearts belong.
Memories in every grain,
Whispered through the window's pane.

Timbered havens, strong and true,
Stand as guardians of the blue.
Here, amidst the forest's keep,
Tales of yore linger deep.

Crafting Nature's Architect

In sylvan glades where rivers wind,
Nature's plans we deftly find.
Architects with hands of grace,
Shape the wild, each time and place.

From bough to beam, a vision's cast,
Crafted sure to ever last.
Wood and stone in harmony,
Blend in perfect symmetry.

Shelters rise beneath the sun,
Warmed by lands where rivers run.
Every grove and hill, a site,
For dreams brought forth by morning light.

Through seasons' change, their forms refine,
Crafted by both hand and time.
Nature's architects compose,
A legacy that gently grows.

In heartwood old, the tale persists,
Of artisans with timeless gifts.
Crafting worlds both wild and grand,
Nature's sculptors, hand in hand.

Sculptors of Silence

In the hush of evening's flow,
Where whispers softly grow,
Artisans of quiet weave,
Dreams the day will not conceive.

With every chisel, tender touch,
They carve the silence much,
In shadows cast by moon's bright glow,
Stories deep within us show.

Their hands so deft, their hearts so pure,
Creating calm that will endure,
Each gentle stroke, a silent speech,
In realms of peace, they dare to reach.

The symphony of stilled breaths,
A quiet night that never rests,
Far from the chaos and the fray,
In silence, sculptors find their way.

They build a world of inner peace,
Where all the noisy clamor cease,
Sculptors of the still, the nighttime's guide,
In silence, all our fears subside.

Water's Edge Engineers

By the banks where willows weep,
They design while others sleep,
Architects of streaming flow,
Crafters of where waters go.

In twilight hours their work takes form,
Though serene, midst chaos swarm,
Rivers bend and curvatures made,
Nature's molds in twilight laid.

Shaping paths with every stone,
Wonders by their hands alone,
Silent builders of dreams immense,
In waters, timeless recompense.

Eddies turn and currents shift,
Underneath their fingers' gift,
Nature's engineers, bold and wise,
In the streams, their blueprints rise.

Their legacy, in ripples cast,
A wondrous tale of futures past,
At water's edge, creation seen,
Engineers weave timeless dream.

Nature's Builders

The ants march forth in single file,
Their paths engrained, mile by mile,
With grains of sand, their homes compile,
Constructing towers in modest style.

Bees take flight from bloom to bloom,
In hives they work, no hint of gloom,
Hexagonal cells, they tightly groom,
A buzzing chorus in summer's plume.

Birds collect from dawn's first light,
Twig and thread in beak's firm bite,
In treetop nests, they softly alight,
Guarding eggs through day and night.

Spiders spin their silken thread,
Fine as whispers, deftly spread,
Their intricate webs a careful spread,
Capturing dreams in twilight's stead.

Termites delve, unseen yet clear,
Timber yields beneath their cheer,
Silent workers, none to sneer,
In grand designs, they persevere.

Nurtured by Nature

A gentle breeze through fields does weave,
Among the leaves, the whispers cleave,
The sun's embrace on a cool reprieve,
Nurtures life where roots believe.

Raindrops kiss the thirsty ground,
A symphony in softest sound,
In forest halls where life is found,
Nature's touch is all around.

Morning dew on petals rest,
In nature's arms, we find our best,
Beneath the sky, our hearts attest,
Life's simple joys are nature-blessed.

The mountains stand in stately rise,
Their peaks reach out to touch the skies,
In shadows cast, where wisdom lies,
Nature's voice in echoes replies.

Oceans vast with waves that sing,
To shores they bring their offering,
In nature's cradle, hearts take wing,
Finding solace in its spring.

Riparian Craftsmen

Beavers carve with paw and tooth,
Banks of rivers, they lift truth,
In dams they build with will and youth,
Riparian gifts in honest proof.

Herons stand in statuesque grace,
Fishing waters, they embrace,
With patience honed, each catch they chase,
Silent poets in nature's space.

Fish weave dances in the stream,
Scales that shimmer, brightly gleam,
Their ripples tell a waking dream,
Flowing threads in nature's seam.

Tall reeds sway with whispered lore,
Where water meets the silty shore,
In rippling waves their secrets pour,
Crafting stories evermore.

Otters play in joyous spree,
The river bends in harmony,
With nimble skill, so wild and free,
True artisans by nature's decree.

Woodland Wonders

Mossy groves in twilight's hush,
Beneath the canopy, green and lush,
A world of wonders that don't rush,
Where time and space begin to blush.

Deer tread softly through the glen,
In silent steps, among the fen,
Their hidden paths unknown to men,
In woodland stories written by pen.

Owls call out in voices deep,
Guardians of the woods they keep,
In moonlit boughs, their secrets seep,
Through shadowed leaves, as forests sleep.

Flowers bloom in colors rare,
In woodland nooks, they paint the air,
With scent and hue beyond compare,
In nature's garden, precious care.

Foxes dart with cunning grace,
In darkened glades they leave no trace,
Their eyes alight in playful chase,
Woodland wonders in silent embrace.

Wildwood Architects

In forested dales where shadows dream,
Whispers of creation softly deem.
Branch by branch, their wonders rise,
Crafted beneath the twilight skies.

With gnarled hands, they weave and bind,
Nature's blueprints in their mind.
Arboreal arches, homes for all,
Silent, green, the leaves' soft call.

Each bough and beam, a story told,
A dance of life, grand and bold.
Antler-touched and paw-trod thread,
Where totem spirits quietly tread.

In glen and grove, their secrets lie,
Architecture kissed by earth and sky.
Humble builders, unsung and true,
Splendor in every morning's dew.

Bound by roots, yet reaching high,
Living spires against the sky.
Crafted chaos, pure design,
Masterpieces, nature's shrine.

Sculptors of the Stream

Down by the water's playful edge,
Dreamers carve in nature's pledge.
Eddies swirl with whispered schemes,
Shaping rills with ancient dreams.

With chisel paws and tooth so keen,
Artisans of the flowing sheen.
Sinuous paths, their opus grand,
Sculpted life from outstretched land.

To twilight's hum and dawn's first rays,
They trace their art in mist and haze.
Rippled songs in liquid run,
Crafting tales of night's begun.

Under moon's reflective gaze,
Their works illuminate the maze.
Contours pressed by starlit beams,
Silent whispers of flowing dreams.

In every current, trace their hand,
Sculpting life from water's strand.
River's heart and stream's soft gleam,
Craftsmen of the endless stream.

Pondside Palaces

Beside the still and mirrored glass,
Builders of the meadows pass.
Crafting homes where ripples play,
Glimpsing life in nature's sway.

Palatial realms on silken banks,
Where lilies nod in quiet thanks.
Reflections dance in water's calm,
A living realm both safe and warm.

With timber beams and mud they mold,
Foundations where their stories hold.
Lattice work of twigs and stone,
Pondside dreams together sown.

Salutary air and tranquil light,
Nestled through the soft moonlight.
Each palace carved by unseen hand,
Whispered touch upon the land.

In this serene and gentle place,
Builders' hearts imbue with grace.
Palaces rise by pond's embrace,
A testament to nature's space.

Wilderness Builders

In realms where wildness roams and reigns,
Builders work with boundless gains.
Nature's blueprint in their paws,
Crafting life with silent laws.

With every twig and leaf they bend,
They shape a world where lives transcend.
Woodland homes from earth and sky,
Born from trails where echoes lie.

Underneath the sylvan veil,
They carve their dreams without fail.
Wilderness as their ancient guide,
A testament deep and wide.

Their handiwork in every tree,
In flowing brook, and bumblebee.
Peers, unseen, yet always there,
In wilderness, their quiet care.

Unsung builders, wild and true,
Crafting worlds in green and blue.
Every leaf and every dawn,
A masterpiece upon the lawn.

Silent Constructions

Beneath the moon's soft, silver glow,
In shadows where cool breezes flow,
Builders work in quiet sheen,
Raising dreams where none have been.

Brick by brick, without a sound,
They craft wonders all around,
Silent hands, with purpose sure,
Creating structures to endure.

Night's contract with dawn waivers,
But these silent, tireless saviors,
With every solemn, humble deed,
Sow seeds for tomorrow's creed.

Stone and timber, earth and sand,
They build with care, by unseen hand,
In the hush of night's embrace,
They carve each corner, line, and grace.

Their art speaks volumes, yet no voice,
Only whispers guide their choice,
Silent constructions stand alight,
Monuments to the quiet night.

Nature's Mason

In forests deep and mountains high,
Where eagles soar and rivers sigh,
Nature's mason crafts in peace,
Works of art that never cease.

With roots to anchor, stone to bind,
Masons of an ancient kind,
Fashioned boundless wonders then,
Calmed by wind and sun again.

Seamless realms where creatures dwell,
In homes that stories softly tell,
Nature molds with gentle hand,
Every hill and every strand.

Winding paths through meadow green,
Lakes reflecting skies serene,
Nature's mason shapes each scene,
Creating realms most unforeseen.

Birds and bees, beneath broad skies,
Live by structures firm and wise,
Crafted by an unseen sage,
Nature's mason of the age.

Streamside Saga

Where the waters softly gleam,
Lives a tale like a dream,
Whispers of the past remain,
Echoes in the flowing lane.

Pebbles speak of days once bright,
Sun-kissed mornings, starry night,
Carved in brook's meandering line,
Tales of old, both yours and mine.

By the stream, the stories mend,
Crafted by the brook's own bend,
Generations whisper low,
In the currents' gentle flow.

Leaves that flutter, roots that hold,
Narrate legends yet untold,
Streamside twists, and time's embrace,
Saga's script on water's face.

From one end to another bound,
History in water's sound,
Streamside keeps its ancient lore,
Saga etched forevermore.

Crafted Currents

In the water's gentle ride,
Crafted currents trace their tide,
Nature carves with liquid grace,
Every turn a soft embrace.

Flowing streams that never still,
Weaving past the ancient hill,
Currents etch their destined run,
Underneath the timeless sun.

Whispers guide the pathways sleek,
Silent shadows that they seek,
Artists of the moving blue,
Painting waves of every hue.

From the crest to valley deep,
Crafted currents climb and leap,
Infinite in their design,
Echoes on the waters' line.

Each new day, a journey cast,
Currents flow both slow and fast,
Crafted by an unseen hand,
A river's dance across the land.

Canopies

Beneath the green and gentle shade,
Where sunlight dances, light delayed,
Lives a world serene and still,
Underneath the forest's will.

Leaves compose a living roof,
Sheltering the earth aloof,
Canopies of dreams and sighs,
Skipping through the azure skies.

Branches weave a ceiling tight,
Safe within the canopy's light,
Nature's fortress, whispering low,
Songs of wind in gentle flow.

Each shadow cast, a painter's brush,
Coloring silence, calming rush,
Underneath the leafy sea,
Incanopies, we find we're free.

Hidden paths, and secret glades,
In the green, each fear fades,
Canopies, the earth's embrace,
Sheltering life in tender grace.

Printed in the USA
CPSIA information can be obtained
at www.ICGtesting.com
LVHW020829030924
789973LV00015B/774

9 789916 864944